SEABOARD AIR LINE RAILWAY

Historic Savannah

Historic Savannah: A 1901 hand-tinted image portrays Savannah more than a century ago, with tall ships docking along the riverfront. Thirty-two feet deep, the length of the river in Savannah provided the largest port in the South. Known as Factor's Row, this section of the riverfront contained many offices and warehouses of companies involved in the cotton trade.

© 2007 Schiffer Publishing Ltd.

schifferbooks.com

Historic Savannah

Historic Savannah: A hand-tinted photo portrays Savannah more than a century ago, with a view of Bull Street as seen from Monterey Square. The streets of Savannah are so beautiful, they have inspired artists and photographers for decades. Savannah's wide streets are lined with majestic architecture, and shaded by live oaks, magnolias, and palm trees.

schifferbooks.com

© 2007 Schiffer Publishing Ltd.

Historic Savannah

Historic Savannah: A hand-tinted photo portrays
Savannah more than a century ago, with a view of
Broughton Street from Bull Street. This is one of the
principal business streets in the city. At this intersec-
tion sits the Oglethorpe Club, today the oldest
gentlemen's club in Georgia. In 1861, it was the site
where the Ordinance of Secession was passed in a
run-up to the Civil War.

schifferbooks.com

© 2007 Schiffer Publishing Ltd.

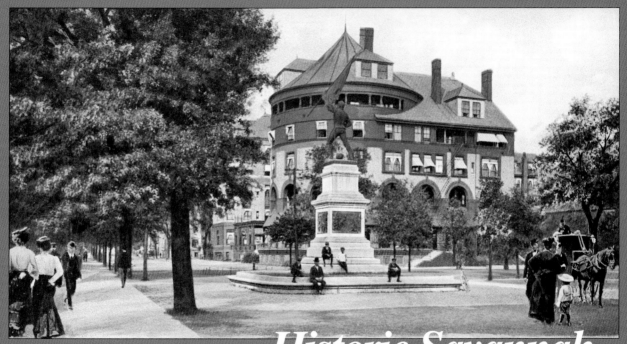

Historic Savannah

Historic Savannah: A hand-tinted photo portrays Savannah more than a century ago, with a view of Madison Square showing the Jasper Monument and the DeSoto Hotel. William Jasper distinguished himself for heroism three times during the Revolutionary War, dying of wounds received during the third feat saving his South Carolina flag from the British during the Second Battle of Savannah. The beautiful DeSoto building was demolished in 1966 and rebuilt as the DeSoto Hilton Hotel.

© 2007 Schiffer Publishing Ltd.

schifferbooks.com

HISTORIC SAVANNAH

Historic Savannah: A hand-tinted photo portrays
Savannah more than a century ago, with a view of
Bull Street looking north toward City Hall. The streets
of Savannah are so beautiful, they have inspired
artists and photographers for decades. Savannah's
wide streets are lined with majestic architecture, and
her business districts have bustled for decades with
the commerce of a busy port town.

© 2007 Schiffer Publishing Ltd.

schifferbooks.com

Historic Savannah

Historic Savannah: A hand-tinted photo portrays
Savannah with a view of Oglethorpe Avenue. This
beautiful stretch of residential street was named for
James Edward Oglethorpe, who arrived in the New
World in February 1733 with a charter from King
George II of England to found the new colony of
Georgia. On the left, the spire of Independent Presbyterian Church rises above the trees. The church was
destroyed by fire in 1889, and since this image was
copyrighted 1900, it portrays the original church and
not the reproduction erected after the disaster.

© 2007 Schiffer Publishing Ltd.

schifferbooks.com

Historic Savannah

Historic Savannah: A hand-tinted photo, copyrighted 1904, portrays Savannah with a view of a Forsyth Park entrance. The promenade leads to the famous Forsyth Park Fountain. Called the Forest City, Savannah is characterized by its abundant natural scenery, and its beautiful parks, squares, and even cemeteries. Forsyth Park was laid out in 1851, and named for John Forsyth who was Governor of Georgia from 1827 to 1829, and Secretary of State from 1834-1841.

© 2007 Schiffer Publishing Ltd.

schifferbooks.com

Historic Savannah

Historic Savannah: A hand-tinted photo captures the Chatham Academy and Independent Presbyterian Church, circa 1915. This Oglethorpe Avenue building, designed by architect Henry Urban, became home to the school in 1908. At one time the school served as the only public high school in Savannah, and is now home to the Savannah-Chatham County Board of Public Education.

© 2007 Schiffer Publishing Ltd.

schifferbooks.com

Historic Savannah

Historic Savannah: A hand-tinted photo portrays Savannah with a view of City Hall, the Green Monument, and the Savannah Bank and Trust Company, circa 1912. City Hall was designed by architect Hyman Wallace Witcover in 1906. Sited on a small bluff overlooking the Savannah River, City Hall sits on the precise spot where city founder James Oglethorpe and his colonists first camped. Initially developed as the site for the City Exchange, it was cleared for redevelopment by a hurricane in the late nineteenth century.

schifferbooks.com

© 2007 Schiffer Publishing Ltd.

Historic Savannah

Historic Savannah: A hand-tinted photo portrays
Savannah with a view of what was called "the
Government Building"and the Courthouse when this
picture was taken circa 1910, and later served as the
post office. Savannah's architecture embraces neo-
classical design elements, creating a sense of the
Old World, combined with the gracious hospitality of
The South.

© 2007 Schiffer Publishing Ltd.

schifferbooks.com

Historic Savannah

Historic Savannah: A hand-tinted photo portrays
Savannah with a view of Union Station, circa 1907.
A trolley car and horse and carriage pre-date the
arrival of the automobile on the scene. Frank P.
Milburn, who also designed Augusta's Union
Station as well as several state courthouses in
Georgia, designed Union Station. It was demolished
in 1962 to make way for an interstate.

© 2007 Schiffer Publishing Ltd.

schifferbooks.com

Historic Savannah

Historic Savannah: A hand-tinted photo, circa 1907, portrays Savannah with a view of one of the city's enduring top sites – Sherman's Old Headquarters. At the end of a great swath of devastation inflicted by Sherman's Army as he laid the Civil War to rest, Sherman arrived in Savannah and declared that preservation of the beautiful city would be his Christmas gift to President Lincoln in 1864. By May the following year, the war had ground to its end.

schifferbooks.com

© 2007 Schiffer Publishing Ltd.

Historic Savannah

Historic Savannah: Automobiles date this hand-tinted photo to the early 1920s. Behind them stands Christ Church, erected on the site of the first church service conducted for the new colony in 1733. Completed in 1750, the church became home to North America's first Sunday School class, taught by the Reverend John Wesley, co-founder of the Methodist denomination with his brother, Charles. The brothers came to Georgia in 1735 with Oglethorpe's second voyage, John as a missionary and Charles as secretary to Governor Oglethorpe.

schifferbooks.com

© 2007 Schiffer Publishing Ltd.

Historic Savannah

Historic Savannah: A hand-tinted photo, circa 1910, portrays Savannah with a view of the Cathedral of St. John the Baptist. It is considered one of the city's most beautiful churches, and one of the largest Roman Catholic Cathedrals in the South. It was designed by architect Francis Baldwin and built in 1872-1876.

© 2007 Schiffer Publishing Ltd.

schifferbooks.com

Historic Savannah

Historic Savannah: A hand-tinted photo, circa 1910, portrays Savannah with a view of Independent Presbyterian Church. The church was as a branch of the Church of Scotland in 1755. John Holden Greene, an architect from Rhode Island, designed the building, modeled after St. Martin's-in-the-Field in London. Woodrow Wilson married Ellen Axson, his first wife, in the manse behind the church in 1885.

schifferbooks.com

© 2007 Schiffer Publishing Ltd.

Historic Savannah

Historic Savannah: A hand-tinted photo, circa 1910, portrays Savannah with a view of First Presbyterian Church on Monterey Square. Thirteen members of the Independent Presbyterian Church founded this church in 1827, the first church in the city to be affiliated with the Presbytery of Georgia. John S. Norris designed the Gothic-inspired building, and though the foundation was laid in 1857, its completion was delayed by the Civil War. Completed in 1872, the church served the congregation until the 1920s. Today it is home to the United Way.

© 2007 Schiffer Publishing Ltd.

schifferbooks.com

Historic Savannah

Historic Savannah: A hand-tinted photo, circa 1910, portrays Savannah with a view of Monterey Square and the Pulaski Monument. A foreign general who had distinguished himself in his native Poland in battles against the Russians, Count Casimir Pulaski became the highest-ranking foreign officer to die in the American Revolution during the Siege of Savannah in 1779. Pulaski's remains were re-interred under the monument in this square in 1854.

schifferbooks.com

© 2007 Schiffer Publishing Ltd.

HISTORIC SAVANNAH

Historic Savannah: The Confederate Monument has towered over Forsyth Park since it was raised in 1875. The figure on top faces north in order to repel the Yankee invaders and the inscription reads "Come from the four Winds O Breath and breathe upon these slain that they may live." The hand-tinted photo, circa 1920, is among many that portray this statue.

© 2007 Schiffer Publishing Ltd.

schifferbooks.com

Historic Savannah

Historic Savannah: A hand-tinted photograph, circa 1920s, portrays one of the favorite destinations for those who visit the Savannah Hermitage Plantation House. The main house at the Hermitage meets the expectation of fans of *Gone With the Wind*, built in the columned Greek Revival Style. The 400-acre plantation on the Savannah River, just north of the city, was built in the 1820s by one of the South's most wealthy men, Henry McAlpin.

© 2007 Schiffer Publishing Ltd.

schifferbooks.com

Historic Savannah

Historic Savannah: A hand-tinted photograph, circa 1920s, portrays the new "million dollar road" built between the city and Tybee Island. The road became the city's entrance to the Ocean, and automobiles made the journey an easy day trip for Savannah's residents and visitors. The beach has been described as Georgia's playground.

© 2007 Schiffer Publishing Ltd.

schifferbooks.com